MULE OF THE WORLD

A collection of poetry, Volume I

By Ayoka B.

Mule of the World

Ayoka B.

Published by Joyinhome Publishing

ISBN: 979-8-9897325-24

To the little girl inside. May she heal.

This is dedicated to all people who have touched my life in both good and not so good ways. I do this because I would not be the person I am or be able to write this book if it weren't for all of these people. To those who have loved, hated, abused, caressed, used, supported and lied to me- this book is written because of and in spite of you.

I think that we want to try and block out or forget all the bad things that happen and all of the people associated. And sometimes, I guess we should for sanity's sake. But, sometimes, we have to embrace it all so that we can learn and grow- know what not to do again, and live. I am not a doctor and my life is far from perfect, but I am strong and I know it's because of going through the chaos. There are, however, those of us who seem to require chaos.

The actual dedication is close to my heart; it is for women. Yes, men can and will enjoy this book. But, I wrote this as an inspiration to women.

Women hold everything together. We have a spirit that is buoyant and most times shatterproof, most times. This book is for strong and happy women and broken and bruised women. This is for rich and poor women. Women with PhDs and GEDs; women who dropped out of school because they felt there were no other options for someone like them. This is for mothers and those who are childless: single, married and widowed. I write this book as a celebration of womanhood and all its inherent blessings and woes.

While this book was written with all women in mind, it is especially for the group to which I belong- black women. I am saddened by the loneliness that I see in so many of my sisters' eyes. I am also saddened by our capacity to hurt each other.

The title of this book, Mule of the World, is a phrase
that I borrowed from author Zora Neale Hurston's
Their Eyes Were Watching God. I read this book for the
first time in high school, I think, again in college and
again as a mature woman. The phrase 'mule of the
world' is her description of black women. I wrote a
poem with the same title during a very painful time. My
blog bears the same name.

Since high school, I have used writing to heal me. It has
continued in spurts and when I needed it most.
Sometimes I awake in the night and words tumble from
my mind, onto waiting pages. So I keep journals beside
my bed. As I said, I wrote this book to inspire: for that
loneliness that I see too often and to deal with what life
has thrown at you. Find your way to work through it.

Themes

From Mom

L-O-V-E

Opinion

Introspection

From Mom

Love Child

I see it in the bow of her legs,
The tightness of her curls.
It's in infectious peals of laughter;
The excitement of a raised eyebrow.

The perfectness of her.

In the wicked of her smile,
The serene look of sleep.
Her mercurial temperament
And gentle heart.

The ultimate symbol of a love forgotten.

Contours of his face,
My bright, almond eyes,
Her cupie-doll lips:
An awesome blend of us
With a uniqueness all her own.

Although the feelings have worn and faded
I see her,
And I am reminded
Of what used to be.

Dinner

Carrots, bananas, sweet potatoes, peas –
What's on tonight's menu?
Carrots it will be...
On hands,
Cheeks,
Eyelashes,
Toes
And me.
Smacking and bouncing show satisfaction,
As she helps me guide the spoon.

I yawn and she is amused.
She has an animated laugh,
Engaging her entire body:
Waving arms
And legs outstretched.
Orange flecks outline her curls,
As the spoon clatters against the empty jar.

The gift

I felt every jab
The flutter of her kicks
And squirms to find a comfortable position.

She suckled my breast
My arm, her cradle.
Snuggled to my chest
And was soothed.

Before breath, she knew me.
My voice,
My heartbeat.

The origin of a father's envy.

He will never know the splendor of birth
Seen through a mother's eyes.

Ode to Tears

Sometimes like a spring rain
We need tears to wash away dirt, debris
Pain...
And to renew and strengthen.
But they never come when I beckon.
A dam was built so long ago
I cannot recall gathering the sticks and mud and leaves
That created the mortar.

Sure, they come during genuine laughter among friends
Or due to the suffering of a child
And sporadically,
Accompanied by white hot anger-
Which cripples reason, no doubt an endearing gift from Dad-
But never when I need them... to cleanse and rebuild.
Upon reflection,
I recall convincing myself that crying provides no solution.
As an adult, I understand their value
Yet they elude me.
Sometimes I think I'm broken...

I want my children to embrace their tears
And understand the strength that they possess.

And so I continue,

My fervent prayer that the well be replenished and restored;

That my heart persuades my mind to give in.

Until then

Like Jay,

I can't see 'em comin' down my eyes

So

I

gotta

make

the

words

c

r

y.

L-O-V-E

She is
Willful and cunning.
She can cause endless regret
And a spring in your step.

She is a plate waiting in the oven
And the feeling that your heart might burst.
She is the lyric in a song,
A giggle during a monotonous chore.
The illogical meshing of two into one.

She is sometimes confused with her sister, Lust
With her desire for soft flesh
And toe sucking.
She is stealthy and comes when your life
Is too full.
She has no regard for time, plans
And sometimes, feelings.

She is a silent tear on a pillow
And an erotic daydream
During a night out.
When determined, she is powerful
And merciless—
Submission is guaranteed.

Her name
Is Love.

Adoration

In your arms, I am safe

Within the warmth of a strong embrace.

Powerful hands, yet a gentle touch

Could be what I love so much.

Your dimpled smile warm like the sun

Lets me know you're the only one

To bring me joy in this world of pain

And bring me laughter through the rain.

That small imperfection on your face,

The passage of time could not erase.

Life's lessons have made you wise

Its secrets hidden behind dark eyes.

Soft, full lips that beckon me

Into your love; set me free.

Long lashes brush against my cheek

And the smooth baritone to make me weak.

Broad shoulders and a muscular back

Ebony skin is my aphrodisiac.

You stroke my hair as I drift to sleep,

And into my dreams you always creep.

Love is you forevermore,

Black man it is you that I adore.

Untitled

I have loved into the depths of my being,
And surrendered my heart and soul without question.
So to settle for relations devoid of meaning,
Why consider the suggestion?

Caresses to make me tremble and shake
These sensations I intensely miss
But an intimate commitment I'll never make
Just because I burn from your kiss.

A smile to make my heart shine
With lips that curl in that sly, sexy way;
I want your body, spirit and mind
Then, in your arms I will lay.

In my heart there is room to spare,
When you yearn for me only.
So until you learn that I don't share,
I don't mind being lonely.

Sounds in the Kitchen

The tinkling of forks hitting a glass
Sudsy water sloshing
Over the lip of the sink,
Saturday morning cartoon music is the background noise
As Diallo laughs with his Dad.
The timbre of his voice echoes
Up to the ceilings
Through the hallway
And reverberates
Within me.
A simple chore of cleaning dishes -
Of plates, glasses, knives
A garlic press and pizza cutter-
Signals the end of raising my children
Alone;
Of dateless nights and
Lonely mornings.
He's doing the dishes so I will sleep in...
Sounds in the kitchen.

Hindsight

Your letter,

Came late that Spring afternoon, as I lounged on the back porch. Warm rays filtered through the screen and bounced off the letter, as I read.

Words...careful words, heavy with sweet memories and bitter regret. Of missing my lips brush against your eyelids and the love that nurtured you like a mother's precious milk.

Now, you are envious that a new love found the smile you stole. I can empathize, because whoever said, "it's better to have loved and lost..." never lost anyone.

But, where was my letter when my tears lasted until the tangerine sun broke through the night? Where was my letter, when you discarded me like a bald tire worn from winters passed?

Because, if you could not treat my heart, with the care it deserves, you should have left it untouched.

xoxo

Opinion

On Beauty

The mirror never lies,
It's simply a reflection through your eyes.
My sister, my sister – can't you see
God made us beautiful,
You and me.
But beauty and love must come from within,
Never hide your full-mouthed grin.
Be happy to be nappy and sport your braids,
Waves and curls
Because every confident, strong woman
Was a confident, strong girl.
Your supple skin tones are flawless
Sun-kissed from head to feet
From French vanilla to mocha java
And just as sinfully sweet.
Be proud of your luscious lips,
Sway your come-hither hips.
Deep, melodic tones when you speak
That render the brothers smitten and weak.

Your package is specially marked "au naturale"
No additives or artificial ingredients necessary.

Sister, to the phenomenal woman you must be true,
Because young sisters are watching, waiting
To be just like you.

The Most Beautiful Shade of All

A cherished indulgence-
The buzz of patron's gossip and the pungent smell of
acetone.
She wore a pink lapel pin, a ribbon.
Beneath her pink baseball cap pecked
Her head:
Smooth and hazel
like a newborn's bottom.
Above the whir of the fans
She chatted,
Lively and inviting.
I wriggled my toes
Hastening the drying process.
This time I chose the blush of a tulip's petal.

Her words, a blur
But crystallized is her aura,
Her personal glow.
Alive, feminine and radiant.

She admired my pedicure.
"That is a beautiful color."
But hers was the most beautiful shade of all.

White Girl

Pink flesh
            Foreign scent
    European flavor

What spell do you cast over my brother?
His mind slips into a state of forgetfulness...
Of melanin
Round ass and hips
Large, soft lips
Sharp tongues and minds
Chocolate babies and ebony eyes.
Is it love that you seek
Or a taste of forbidden fruit, now the catch du jour?
I can't say that I blame you.
But,
I warn you...
Respect his touch
Love his mind
Cherish his future
Because,
There is always a sista,
To nurse him back
To health.

Trigger Happy

Pop-

Pop, pop, pop, pop, pop, pop!

Silence...

No siren.

No special report to follow.

Blood,

That has been

Mutilated,

    raped,

       degraded,

         lynched

Has survived

With pride, strength, anger and love

To be spilled on a

Dark street

A nameless alley.

Staccato breaths

Gasp for air,

Help,

Hope.

My heart is torn.

I hate you

For hating him

And yourself.

But I love you.

What can I do to show you?

Introspection

Masterpiece

You made me over in your image.
I was but a reflection of you.

Virgin clay, molded with care.
Your skillful eye gave me grace,
Strength and poise.
Your gifted hands formed the intricacies of my being,
And sculpted my femininity.
Before the artist, I was but virgin clay.

Your devotion breathed life into my body
And warmth into my heart.
Alive, and my soul danced for you-
A masterpiece, behold her beauty!

But suddenly,
The artist is gone
Never to witness his creation.
And I stand,
Unfinished.

Loneliness

Is silent nights lost in the pages of strangers' lives.
It is the absence of five-year old hugs
offering unconditional love from a clean heart.

Is a quiet house-
no low moans
Before the morning routine.

Is longing for a heart to match your rhythm
Of dreams and laughter.

Is snapshots of watercolor memories that fade
Like a forgotten picture show.

Loneliness,
Is getting used to
Being alone.

Unknown

Do you know my favorite color?
Favorite food?
Do you know what makes me happy? Sad?
What is the meaning of my name?

Do you know my intelligence
Or sassy way?
Do you know
What I choose not to say?
Can you tell what I'm thinking
By the glint in my eye?
Did you know that I love real hard
And trust very little?

Treasure what I give.
Love me when I'm not looking.
Listen to what I offer.
To know me, is to love me...
Even the rough parts.

Someone told me that I was hard to know-
Maybe,
Nobody has ever tried.

Ode to the Single Mother

One does not aspire to be a single mother.

As a young girl, I did not look into the mirror and long to follow in my mother's footsteps. In fact, I was hopeful that I would raise my children in a household with two, loving parents.

But in the absence of that picture,

what can I say to you to lighten your load?

And ignite that twinkle in your eye that far too often loses its luster-

The road can be lonely, sometimes weary but punctuated with snaggletoothed smiles and "I love yous" with tiny arms encircling your tired neck.

Remember that you are not a bad word or cautionary tale;

Not a stereotype or reason for shame- leave that for silent fathers to claim.

Realize that you will know love although it may not happen the way you thought it would...

Or when you think it should.

Keep love at the center of your family.

Show your children, better than you can tell them.

It's okay to think about yourself once in a while.

I am proud of some of my sisters that heard tick, tock of their clock

And chose to follow their heart's desire over

Loose lips, barrenness or a bad marriage.

A little support would be nice- no not a handout- a kind, supportive word

To break the monotonous cycle of school/work/motherhood.

An acknowledgment that right or wrong,

We are single-handedly raising many of the next generation.

Sister-

Know that God counts your tears and

We see you.

Keep your head up.

Smile.

One day your son (or daughter) could be president.

Reflection

I looked in the mirror today
And guess what I saw?
A beautiful woman.

I looked closer
To see what others must.
Something,
Anything that would explain...
Your willingness to bask in my devotion,
While quietly watching my heart break
Into fragments at your feet.

I looked to see if there were traces
Of the salty tears
Wasted
On someone who could dismiss my feelings
So easily.

I looked one last time
For signs of a fool
For the weak person that they must see.
All I saw was a beautiful woman.

Reflection

I looked in the mirror today
And guess what I saw?
A beautiful woman.

I looked closer
To see what others must.
Something,
Anything that would explain...
Your willingness to bask in my devotion,
While quietly watching my heart break
Into fragments at your feet.

I looked to see if there were traces
Of the salty tears
Wasted
On someone who could dismiss my feelings
So easily.

I looked one last time
For signs of a fool
For the weak person that they must see.
All I saw was a beautiful woman.

Mule of the World

I see her often,

That young woman with sad, troubled eyes.

Her vacant stare looks through me.

What troubles her so?

She was once a strong, black woman!

But the world has made her weak.

So weak,

That sometimes, she doesn't feel she can hold on.

But what does she have

To hold onto?

Pain and loneliness are her only companions.

So many thoughts

Of love and joy swirl through her mind

Like watercolors, beautiful colors...

They are far away.

She is lost

Or maybe she has lost her mind.

And so she writes,

Because you see the pen is mightier than the sword

Or so someone once said.

Still her pain is dry and hot like the blue of a flame

And burns from within.

Eyes are the windows of the soul

The ugliness of the world is reflected in those empty
eyes.

Because as Zora said, "the black woman is the mule of
the world."

The doormat of society, the scapegoat of her
community.

Eyes of a young, black woman.

If you look closely, you will see they are mine.

Ayoka B. explores the themes of Womanhood, identity, love, loss and family through poetry, fiction and nonfiction. Her writing is vulnerable and honest which resonates with readers. Through her unique lens as a Black woman and DC native, Ayoka seeks to share the untold stories of mothers, sisters, daughters, friends and wives. Her goal is to help people gain clarity and insight into their lives.

Ayoka has a professional background in public relations and strategic communications. She received a bachelor's degree in Communications from Temple University in Philadelphia, Pa. and a master's degree in Public Communication from American University in Washington, DC. Ayoka is a mother and lives with her family in Costa Rica.

This is the first poetry collection in a series of four books. Her debut novel, *Love At Second Sight*, published in 2024. Learn more at linktr.ee/joyinhome